T0071740

ALSO BY DEVIN JOHNSTON

POETRY

Traveler

Sources

Aversions

Telepathy

PROSE

Creaturely and Other Essays

*Precipitations: Contemporary American
Poetry as Occult Practice*

FAR-FETCHED

Far-Fetched

DEVIN JOHNSTON

FARRAR STRAUS GIROUX

NEW YORK

Farrar, Straus and Giroux

18 West 18th Street, New York 10011

Library of Congress Cataloging-in-Publication Data

Johnston, Devin.

[Poems. Selections]

Far-fetched : poems / Devin Johnston. — First edition.

pages ; cm

ISBN 978-0-374-53670-1

ISBN 978-0-374-71408-6 (e-book)

I. Title.

PS3610.O385 A6 2015

811'.6 — dc23

2014031266

Designed by Quemadura

Farrar, Straus and Giroux books may be purchased for
educational, business, or promotional use. For information
on bulk purchases, please contact the Macmillan Corporate and
Premium Sales Department at 1-800-221-7945, extension 5442,
or write to specialmarkets@macmillan.com.

www.fsgbooks.com
www.twitter.com/fsgbooks
www.facebook.com/fsgbooks

P1

From hence the River fetches a large Winding . . . —Benjamin Martin

CONTENTS

FAR-FETCHED

AMERAUCANA

Well, Sally Hen, how do you like your home?
A straight run from the east to the west
with hardscrabble fit for a choral dance
and overhead, a walnut tree,
lord of ice and obstacles.

In the morning dark or dusk of an afternoon,
you softly cluck, then settle down
to roost in mercury-vapor light
with spring behind your lids.

At its first true intimations,
you bend on backward knees
to crop a tussock of cloverleaf,
raising a lateen tail above the trough.

Tufted auriculars disregard
horn and drums, mahogany tones
of a tenor deep within the house,
but not the soft chromatic descent
of snowmelt, or a breath of wind.

From a fallow bed, so much undone,
your parched and reptilian cry proclaims
a perfect form of incompletion:
first egg of the year.

ABOVE IVANHOE

Above Ivanhoe and Fries,
blues dissipate the ridge
as rain comes
wrapped in itself.
Pull the curtain so I can sleep.
A colt's tail drags a scuff,
a handbreadth of cloud
skiffing across the gap,
its wake a drow of cold breath,
a mug of dirty light, tipping out
reflections from a daguerreotype,
smur that deepens and deepens,
turning as smoothly as dusk
from mull to rug
bickering on the chimney cowl.
Socked in, you lie awake
inside a steady rustle,
a sound as dull
and absorbing as paper.

The general condition
leaves a thousand tokens,
hissing in the grate,
swamping the clay chimneys
crayfish make in secret hollows,
lifting oil from asphalt
on the road to Poplar Camp,
dripping from the eaves
of Boiling Springs Baptist Church,
rattling down through
long-abandoned lead mines.

Light pursues each instance,
catching what it can.
A frog pond of pewter.
The dull shine of hair.
At the ferry crossing,
broad and shallow,
a chain still glints
beneath the spangled current.

Later, along the ridge,
a few lamps shine
through tent canvas,
the woods around them writhing.

FAR-FETCHED

Six hundred feet above the dam at Fries
a stony pasture buckles across the top
and dips toward Austinville.
In a kettle, buzzards
glide at ease
on the river's steam,
up and up
through clockwise turns until
they catch a whiff of rot
and give chase
at a tightrope-walking pace,
no hurry, prey already caught.

Vibrations carry the faintest ring
of metal struck on metal, a cattle bell,
a corrugated pipe
through which a breath
might oscillate and sing,
a rough staccato
bark or yell,

faint as the *chip chip chip*
sweet-sweet-sweet sweeter-than-sweet
from a yellow warbler's throat.
An engine flutters, remote,
and the crunch of gravel softens in retreat.

Two horses, hard to bridle, watch the road.
Another sleeps in shade beside a shed,
hock-deep in poison ivy.
Among its vines
bedsprings corrode
and blacksnake
breeds with copperhead.
You seen a river puppy,
down by the waterside?
They got the teeth of chillern
and fur that fire can't burn,
but human reek they can't abide.

As gravel thins, the road becomes a track
that climbs through cloud and sunlight, lead and zinc.
The ruts have overgrown
and cede to scrub,
with no way through or back.
At this remove

a couch and a kitchen sink
have come to rest where thrown
in thick Virginia poke,
far from any route
you'd take in setting out
from Bristol, Boone, or Roanoke.

THE CLYDE

We took your name from firth and river
that you might go forth and meander

from narrow waters of your birth
across the surface of the earth

and take such windings to and fro,
each scribble unconstrained yet slow,

each stroke and shallow stream of babble
transumptive, *metonymical*,

the idle tracing of a mood
with purposeless exactitude

that curls now on a backward course
and almost seems to reach the source

but turns away eventually
to join the firth and open sea.

A FLY FROM THE EARLY ANGLERS

In August, on a hot day,
walk by the Tweed and mark what falls
on the water, in some quiet place,
beneath a bridge, above a bed
of sand or gravell, wherever a Trout
lies boldly gleaming neer the top
and keeps watch for a wrinckle
betwixt him and the skie.

Take a brass-plate winding reele,
and for your line, five horses hayres,
and for your flye, a Cloudie Darke
of wooll clipt from betweene the eares
of sheepe, and whipt about with silk,
his wings of the under mayle of the Mallard,
his head, made black and suitable,
fixed upon a peece of corke
and wrapt so cunningly round the hooke
that nothing could betray the steele
but a hint of poynt and beard.

At no time let your shadow
lye upon the water
or cause a stone to clap on stone.
Be stil, and smoothly draw your flye
to and fro in a kind of daunce
as if it were alive.

SHROOMS

He learned to read before the rest of us
and rose to the highest stream by six,
a reedy laugh above the din of voices.
Before dawn, waiting for the bus,
he stooped to pluck a shaggy parasol
and offered it to me, a boutonniere
from the wrong kingdom, a different form of life.
I didn't know him well, you understand.

At fifteen, but for an earthy musk
and army coat, he left the world
and entered a circle of silence.
Survived by delivering pizzas, dealing pot.
Prepared nothing, confiding in no one,
why I never knew, with none to ask.

After twenty years, I could still find him
living here, lodged in his mother's basement,
shooting pool and breathing through his gills,
inhaling the base notes of wet dog,

woolen afghan, and stale tobacco.
Small fears bloom through lethargy
like mushrooms through their universal veils.
Should he emerge from his cul-de-sac
and over Silas Creek, autumnal sunlight
snapping at his face, caught in his lashes,
he might well give a sign of recognition,
tipping a phantom cap sardonically
with the furtive look of a poacher on his rounds.

PUFFBALL

Beside a richly
rotting oak
a moon fruits forth,
a tender moon
about the size
of a human head,
of the earth
yet nothing like it.

If you pass
this way at dusk,
bring it home
in a paper bag,
light and full
as a thought bubble,
enough, enough
to displace
whatever you had
in mind.

SATURDAY MORNING

Regret the time
wasted on work
which finds you
even here
but not hachures
of steep ascent
or the unremitting need
for learning facts
and calculating
unresolved events
ripples at the edge
of an ancient sea
Liesegang rings
from water and iron
corrugations
of unclenched surface
graffiti
light as lines
from a graphite pencil

scribbled around
a medallion of lichen
absorbing the sun

Wind and rain
go on eroding
hoodoo from bluff
the mutable form
of horse or mushroom
loaf or anvil
a cloven god
unresolved
and self-absorbed
in slow collapse
back to the clastic bed
and hoof clatter
just beyond
an ice sheet's
leading edge

GEODE

In a farmhouse at dusk,
a young girl sorts her rocks
and stores them in a cardboard box
where they nestle in tissue paper,
at rest from erosion.

Her fingers, soft as tissue,
lift and turn a geode
(the accident of epochs)
as if it were an egg.
For her, the stone is new.

THE SOUTHERN

An oval fob of brass,
key still attached,
surfaced in a shop on Cherokee
and now rests atop my desk
beside a small obsidian axe.
Absently, I rub my thumb
across the fob and feel
Southern Hotel, Room 306.
The elegant lobby survives
in a few steel engravings:
palms and spindleback chairs,
fruit in thick cut glass,
men loafing in spats.
One of them slips next door
for a quick nip
and winds up slugging down
half a dozen oysters the size of eggs,
rummaging through the shells.
Amidst the bright din
of cutlery and chatter,

the whiskey—a second, then a third—
encourages equilibrium,
then a calm indifference.
The evening sun goes down,
drawing river smells
through shadows of the Sixth Ward,
blushing the hotel's stone façade,
enflaming its westward-facing rooms.
Behind the front desk, a plaque
commemorates Chief Pontiac,
leader of the Ottawa
and great friend to Louisiana,
buried in a blue coat
beyond the cemetery gates,
no one knows quite where.

A CLOSE SHAVE

From Baden, or what's left of it,
pursue a long, smooth curve of road
that skirts the northern flood wall
to parallel a palisade
of channel markers sunk in earth,
the folly of a cement works.
Its blank silos overlook
a pit of argillaceous shale,
the fine and fossilized remains
of bivalves, sponges, spines of shark,
quarried and burnt with limestone charge
to alchemize a binder of brick
and the city's shallow, brittle crust.

Around a bend, the riverbed
swings wide to open a fetch of field.
Shadows skim its mucky thaw
as juncos, whisked about by the wind
on courses neither fixed nor free,
give but a quick metallic chink.
Behind you, rain has wrapped the bluffs

and scumbled limbs of sycamores.
Ahead, each bend assumes the name
of a gaudy packet run aground,
or snagged and sunk, or blown to bits:
for one, the side-wheel *Amazon*,
pluperfect wheelhouse painted green,
that struck a honey-locust pike
still rooted deep in river mud
and tore its hull from stem to stern.
Down in minutes! Within the month
an island silted up behind.

A flock of luggage floated south,
remarked by those on Water Street
loafing before the trading post
and the barbershop of Madame Krull.
She can *eternally* be found
at work in her elaborate room
toujours prête to clip and coif
or wield her razor with great skill
for those who favor her with their chins.
The scent of ginger tonic blends
with that of borscht, its acrid tang,
consumed behind a wooden screen
as Illinois grows dark. In this,
her second year since coming west.

ORPINGTONS

A pair of Orpingtons,
one blue, the other black,
with iridescent necks
and fine, ashen fluff
cackle through the dark,
their damp calls close enough
to chafe, a friction with no spark.

They settle down to roost,
two rests along a stave.
Each curls into itself,
comb tucked beneath a wing,
as the days grow long enough
to kindle in each a yolk,
the smallest flame of spring.

NEW SONG

after William IX, Duke of Aquitaine

As sweetness flows through these new days,
the woods leaf out, and songbirds phrase
in neumes of roosted melody
incipits to a new song.
Then love should find lubricity
and quicken, having slept so long.

The bloodroot blossoms, well and good,
but I receive no word that would
set my troubled heart at ease,
nor could we turn our faces toward
the sun, and open by degrees,
unless we reach a clear accord.

And so our love goes, night and day:
it's like the thorny hawthorn spray
that whips about in a bitter wind

from dusk to dawn, shellacked with sleet,
until the sun's first rays ascend
through leaves and branches, spreading heat.

I have in mind one April morning
when she relented without warning,
relenting from her cold rebuff
in laughter, peals of happiness.
Sweet Christ, let me live long enough
to get my hands beneath her dress!

I hate the elevated talk
that disregards both root and stalk
and sets insipid pride above
vicissitudes of lust and strife.
Let others claim a higher love:
we've got the bread, we've got the knife.

SYRINX

Just a glimpse
of rufous thatch
and curved bill

a brown thrasher

flipping up
wood chips
at the water's edge

scuttles through sumac
and shakes the hedge
with oscillations

Panic constricts
the double syrinx

water reeds
bound with wax

goad and goaded
again and again
toward improvisation

chelping a wet
couplet through ceramic

licentious yet pure

yellow eye
disinterested
witness to the song

TELEPHONE

A mockingbird
perched on the hood
of a pay phone
half buried in a hedge
of wild rose
and heard it ring

The clapper ball
trilled between
brass gongs
for two seconds
then wind
and then again

With head cocked
the bird took note
absorbed the ringing
deep in its throat
and frothed
an ebullient song

The leitmotif
of bright alarm
recurred in a run
from hawk
to meadowlark
from May to early June

The ringing spread
from syrinx to syrinx
from Kiowa
to Comanche to Clark
till someone
finally picked up

and heard a voice
on the other end
say *Konza*
or *Consez* or *Kansa*
which the French trappers
heard as *Kaw*

which is only the sound
of a word for wind
then only the sound of wind

TEMPERS

Hot days, violent storms,
high clouds, cold rain.

*

Sheets and curtains cast
a white-diamond gloom.

Are you asleep?

Wind heaves
against the glass

and slow breathing
fills the room.

*

Soft pillows, soft
blankets, soft sheets:

Her kiss? Sweet,
and hard enough
to crack your teeth.

*

Dark at noon
and darker still
beneath a tossing oak

where subaquatic
light renders
ironwork remote.

*

Clouds purl
in a conch whorl

around a center
yet to be declared.

CIRCLE LINE: LONDON

Curve of recurrence

Horns of dawn

Wheels touch down
on the smooth
ceremonial runway

a grand plaza
of stenciled arrows
to and from the sky

*

Soft clatter of plates
Clack of rain coming on

Her head sunk
in a leather menu

Her white fingers
turn a fork

and harrow the tablecloth
with tines

*

At the Electric Cinema
a hand waits its turn
outside a bag of popcorn

*

Browsing through a bookshop's
narcotic dusk
she comes across
an aquatint
of brook trout
in the bargain cellar
submerged from street life

Day slips past

*

Stout and tobacco smoke

Tail end of a head cold

Bespattered pigeon cote

*

A bathtub
brindled with rust
glows in the dusk

Her white knee
sleek as a seal
breaks the surface

Estuaries
overflow
across the tile

TWO FROM CATULLUS

1

You ask how many kisses
would leave me satisfied?
As many as the grains of silt
that flow from Alton south
across the wide
Missouri's mouth,
as many as the stars that shine
through quiet August nights
on tangled forms
of humankind,
so many kisses might
leave this craving satisfied—
more kisses than the curious
could tabulate
or bitter tongues malign.

Lizzie, you once said
I knew you as no other did
and that you'd rather lie in my arms
than in the light of Jesus.
I loved you then, not
as most men do their women,
but as a father loves his children.

These days I know you better,
and though I'm more
aroused by your touch,
you flaunt and flutter
through my thoughts
without much hold.
You wonder how this happened?

Such betrayal as yours excites
more desire and less affection.

BRIGHT THORN

Excrucior,
the crux of it:
torn between
two states of mind,
the axes of
a new life
and of the one
you left behind.
Time and time
again, you learn
nothing but pain
from pain.
Behind the school
each bright thorn
collects
a bead of rain.

GLOSS

Not long before your tongue
flutters inside *my* mouth,

nimble tip searching out
something to be said,

just as the deaf and blind
brush hands in tactile signs.

VISITING DAY

Do not share food or drinks.
No rubbing arms or touching faces.
Visitors and offenders may
hold hands across the table.
You will only be permitted
one greeting and departing kiss,
a closed-mouth kiss
of one to two seconds.
Do not leave children unattended.

FIXED INTERVAL

When he turns fifteen, you'll be fifty-four.
When he turns thirty, you'll be sixty-nine.
This plain arithmetic amazes more
than miracle, the constant difference more
than mere recursion of father in son.
If you reach eighty, he'll be forty-one!

The same sun wheels around again, the dawn
drawn out and hammered thin as a copper sheet.
When he turns sixty, you'll be gone.
Compacted mud, annealed by summer heat,
two ruts incise this ghost-forsaken plain
and keep their track width, never to part or meet.

MEANS OF ESCAPE

The courtroom, clad in wood veneer,
could be a lesser pharaoh's tomb
equipped for immortality.
A civil servant drags her broom
around the bench and gallery
as jurors darken a questionnaire.

One coughs against the courtroom chill.
One drums her fingers atop the bar.
One finds escape through Stephen King,
as through a window left ajar.
One talks and talks, a reckoning
of who got sober, who took ill.

The talker seeks me out at lunch,
a bond of passing circumstance.
He slides the food around his tray
disdainfully and looks askance
at those nearby, as if to say,
In here, you can't expect too much.

Across the hall, five years ago,
the talker fought for custody
and lost, his daylight blotted out.
He'd spent the decade carelessly
and sucked a mortgage up his snout.
He never sees his daughter now.

They meet online for Realms of Ra
as siblings, catlike humanoids,
survivors from the Hybrid Age;
or Foxen riding flightless birds
across the plain, a scrolling page
above which two moons light their way.

They gather gold coins as they roam,
and relics, sometimes holy ones.
They seldom map attentively,
but swing their swords and have some fun.
They chat—backchannel strategy,
but not of school, her friends, or home.

Last night, they entered a castle keep
infested with the living dead,
whose breath abruptly turned the air
to crackled glass. A pop-up read,
Initializing Griffin's Lair:
please wait, and soon he fell asleep.

Of course, he can reboot the game
tonight, with nothing lost or missed.
Meanwhile, a case of larceny
awaits, from which we'll be dismissed
(we both have too much history).
I wish him well in his campaign.

STRANGERS

On an overbooked flight from Houston,
I find my seat beside a woman
in black shades, with the hard-bitten look
that sometimes follows addiction,
nails chewed down to the quick,
talking too loudly into her phone:
Yeah, I got my dad a new amp.
Rocking must run in the family!
As we level off in the tenuous dusk,
she orders a Red Bull and Skyy,
scarfing down her portion of pretzels,
shifting abruptly from side to side
to cross and recross her legs,
swiping through files on her phone.
Meanwhile, I skim an Audubon guide
and pause at the boat-tailed grackle
with its iridescence, yellow eye,
and long, harsh trilling song.
You like that book? she interrupts.
I got some crazy shit to show you.

Here, a silky fantail
from the State Fair of Texas.
Have you ever seen a mule pull?
This team's dragging five tons.
Oh, that's me, getting an award.
I'm a doctor, you believe that shit?
In the snapshot, she wears a white lab coat
with a ribbon pinned to her lapel,
her arm around a soldier's waist
in what looks to be a shopping mall.

I love birds! So check it out:
I raised fuckin' racing pigeons
with my dad, a top geneticist
at Baylor—total brainiac.
We banded squabs, flew them in batches,
drove them out for training tosses.
This one, with a Belgian pedigree,
came first in the Texas Showdown.
Fuckin' A, I loved those birds.

On and on, an improbable mix
of tough talk and expertise
that finds no resolution.
But then, consider my own account,

withheld: an invitation
to read my poetry aloud,
tequila and a fine *lechón*,
a morning free to watch a pair
of caracaras take apart
the carcass of a wild hog
along the Chocolate Bayou.
What would such scraps mean to her?

Even in our final descent
she pushes past my doubt
and reticence, to say,
I started as a dancer,
and now I'm a goddamn doc.
Looking back, it all makes sense!
—the incidents of a life
fanning out in a strange display.

NIGHT AND DAY

Newly a father, half asleep
between the dark and dawn,
I lean against the kitchen sink
and struggle to recall
a riddle of the sphinx,
the western sky a color
that the Greeks refused to name
because it extinguishes all others,
their sea of green or wine,
their sky of hammered bronze.
What starts as a faint
migration of light
extends itself alone and widely
across the kitchen tile,
pewter on a soap bubble,
bombycinous, endored,
adding word to word until
everything gets remembered.
There are two sisters: one
gives birth to the other
and then is born from her.

OWL-EYED

A golden hand
imprints the dawn

figurative
intent forgot

A black jug
with beak and brow

returns the owl
face to Pallas

Countless broken
pots unearth

evidence
of deep thirst

an afterlife
in earthenware

three thousand years
of twilight

THE SUDDEN WALK

after Franz Kafka

When evening comes to find you still
at home and settling down to stay,
when the last rays have lit a cloud
of fingerprints on the storm door
and television's lambent flame
plays across veneer and glass,
when you have dealt a hand or two,
the dinner dishes cleared away,
and shrugging on the familiar robe,
you open an atlas of the world
to archipelagoes engraved
with light of other longitudes,
when a cold fog descends and drives
every creature down its hole,
when you have sat so quietly
that your least movement brings surprise
to everyone, and when, besides,
the stairs are dark, the deadbolt locked,

and in spite of all, you start up
in a sudden fit of restlessness,
shed your robe, snap a coat,
and bang the door shut more or less
emphatically, according to
the pique you fancy having stirred,
and when you find yourself once more
at unexpected liberty,
absorbed in rhythms of breath and limb,
attention racing on ahead
and then returning like a dog
through hawthorn blooming in the dark,
that rich potentiality,
when Mars and Jupiter ascend
above the cloudbank, bright and crisp,
then you become a clean stroke
of ink-and-brush calligraphy,
a lone figure strolling west
on Shenandoah Avenue.

Returning home, still full of such
euphoria, you stop to watch
flitting across your window shade
at this late hour, the silhouettes
of children loosed from all constraints.

TURNED LOOSE

On Friday afternoon, turned loose
like cattle dogs across a slope,
kids fling themselves out of doors
with a thin shout as though through bronze,
descend on idling cars en masse,
and then disperse on separate paths
as we distinguish one of ours.

On Saturday, stunned by the week
of school and work, we rise late
and linger at the table
above the morning's residue
of orange peels and magazines.
Light and unobtrusive,
a pencil rustles paper
to sketch a horse with arched neck
and whipping lines for legs.
Does anybody have the red?

On Sunday, after small delays—
the ritual of a coat refused
or shoe misplaced—we find ourselves
within the hall of mastodons,
our clothes still radiating cold.
We scrutinize an arc of tusk
and chronicle of bone.
Among so many strangers,
the children cling to me like burrs
and I disregard the impulse
to be free of them.

Monday in my office,
a day that will not bring them near,
I want nothing but their presence,
my ears attuned to outdoors
and the timbre of their voices,
the damp friction of their shrieks
so primitive and freshly peeled.

WANT

Let the child cry awhile
with a rasp that strains his throat.

Let him learn what can't be satisfied
and break him like a colt.

Beneath a blanket, let him find
some solace in himself.

*

I need mine cuddy!
—the family word
for a blanket frayed
to a snarl of yarn,
a mushy cud
that smells of spit.

As the soporific
takes effect,
eyes roll inward

and night unravels
the wale
that day has knit.

*

Tilt this lacquered disk
against the sun

tap tap
its pendulum

pulls each head in turn
to pivot in a slot

and peck at painted
flecks of scratch

the hollow tap
of appetite

SCHOOL DAYS

Passing our porch, a girl of ten
holds a drum against her stomach
as you might a covered dish.
China trembles with a truck's idle
or the white hum of compressors,
the morning air muted
as though near the ocean,
lightly ruffled by subaquatic
scales on a clarinet
and the tuning of strings.

When she passes again, near dusk,
the insect chorus subsides
to a pinprick of cricket song.
Narrow pens of fenced yards,
as yet unraked, lie thick
with indotherms and agitrons.
Something keeps brushing against me!

Around a plot of ragged mint,
the lemon zest of walnut leaves
illuminates the lawn,
brickwork slowly revealed.

LATE OCTOBER

Kids crowd the stoop
backs to a darkened house

so close to nothing
yet incurious

*

Across the brick façade
a kestrel

races to meet
its shadow

*

Hawk and starling sport
through all this rigging
of blocks and lines
counterweights and arbors

the street
a theater set for storms

*

A chunk of sycamore
adorns the telephone line
branch and trunk long gone
stump a faint impression

just that cylinder
faintly nautical
hung in a crown of air

*

Triple your chances to win
Take it at twenty-to-one
No money down

No faith in desire

*

Cashing out
the bartender croons
If you see me getting smaller

Trobar clus
Closing time

*

Two boys lug
a Samsonite
full of leaves
across the lawn

*

A starling whets
her thorn of beak

and song gives way
to sunlight on concrete

LEAVING HOME

after Eudora Welty

One beech within a winter wood
glowed with a crown of leaves
and slid behind the bare trees,
a little evening sun.

It traveled with you awhile
in ghostly fashion,
your own crown of hair
in faint reflection,
here and gone.

COME AND SEE

A Sunday in Saint Louis,
the avenues
quiet as country lanes.
Cabbage whites
ride a current of air.
Sycamores lean
and scrape the sky
like schooners
not yet under sail,
their leaves in tatters.
A soft rustle,
a nautical creak.
More faintly still,
sticks clatter
on the playing field
behind Our Lady of Sorrows.
You've lived here
thirty, forty years.

Suddenly a Clydesdale
with no tack or rider
clip-clops around the corner
and trots along
the yellow lines.
A marvel of
the Pleistocene,
creature of grass and dung,
it must have wandered far
to reach us,
through all hours
and seasons,
trampling the dust
of every kingdom.
From dark recesses
residents
step out to watch,
stepping away
from busy lives,
something on the stove,
a bath drawn,
the phone covered
like an astonished mouth.

SMALL TRIUMPHS

Along the freight yard, a cop
waved me to the side.
Windows down, engine off,
I heard the clink of chains
and steady brush of pads
before a pair of elephants
entered my left mirror.

*

A lyrebird at noon!—
fossicking for worms.
No song, no *éventail plissé*
of filaments and plumes.
Regardless, clear as day—
a lyrebird at noon!

*

You talk with animation
of what you've seen, and where—
proud to have been so lucky,
amused to feel so proud.

IN SEARCH OF MULLOWAY

for Bob Adamson

The fisherman makes an appointment
by map and tidal chart
unfolded across the bare floor.
Sorting through his gear,
he ties a knot and talks of jewies,
not jew- but jewelfish
for the otolith within its ear,
a bob for equilibrium
like the bubble of a spirit level.

According to lore, a traveler shines
from weeks on the open sea,
cold sluicing along its flanks
and buffing its soft scales to chrome,
crossing Lord Howe Rise,
who knows why,
then home past Lion Island's head
with a worm inhaled en route
writhing in its gut.

All the while, a resident
turns to bronze and tarnishes
at the mouth of Mooney Creek,
wolfish yet asleep
in the shadow of a pile.
Motionless, the monster steeps
in its own ammonia tang.
Traveler and resident,
both taste about the same.

SAILING UNDER STORM

after Horace

This heavy weather drives you out
to sea once more, old sloop.
What can you do but lie ahull
or run off under bare poles
while trailing lines astern?
Don't you feel your steering fail
and hear your cracked mast groan
in another gust of spindrift,
the night sea full of foam,
and wonder how your hull
could ever survive the coming wave?
You have no seam unsplit, nor God
to call upon in such misfortune.
Though you were built from live oak
and longleaf Georgia pine,
and proudly christened *A-OK*,
the frightened sailor finds
no comfort in a name.

Take care, or you'll become
the laughingstock of wind.
Source of all my drudgery
and now my deep concern:
stay well clear of the hidden reef
from which no ships return.

SILVER

I am the warper
caught in a weir
like a muscular tongue
against the teeth
or stuck with a spear
or reeled from the dark
to writhe on a hook
and make no sound
though sometimes heard
to whistle off-key
in a ruffled sound
or estuary

I am the warper
sniffing the air
and sliding across
rough wood and root
en route to pools
of Ira-waru
or branching streams

of Batasuna
though never at home
in the Pyrenees
preferring the deep
and rolling seas

I am the warper
pickled in brine
a cable wrapped
in gutta-percha
walloping north
as a spring unwinds
its subtle ribbon
beneath the keel
in a warp of murky
light and water
here and gone
a silver eel

TING

A whipbird calls through fog
Its whistle sustains and clarifies
until a crack
taut and metallic
punctuates the morning

Across the estuary
an inlet of the Tasman Sea
bellbirds swing their heads
to ventriloquize
a lip of glass
By channels of coolness
the echoes are calling

each call a drop of water
or tap on glazed ceramic
or *tink* of sonar
to sound the empty space
and test how long

how far
tink tink-ting
tink tink-ting

Think of Ming brushwork
and how each island
has its *ting*
open to all weather
a pavilion in which to pause
among eroded rocks
and cataracts of moss
along a river
still unscrolling

Just so the *tink* of bellbirds
unchanging yet arrhythmic
cool yet intimate
gathers fog around it
to sound the hush
and make it ring

SCAVENGER

A rail, buff-banded rail,
weaves among the legs
of picnickers who loll at ease
on the buttress roots of fig trees.
It queries fallen fruit
with manners so refined
as to be indeterminate,
its herringbone immaculate.
Aloof though underfoot,
the rail extracts a crust
of pie from picnic residue—
no seediness, no trace
of table-scrap solicitude
for any human hand or face.

SATIN BOWERBIRD

Devout in your compulsion,
you weave a bower of endless night
from something old and something new,
collecting bits of broken glass
from a bottle of Bombay Sapphire gin,
a single curl of dyed wool,
parrot feathers, and filaments
from your own electric eye.

Behind a palisade of twigs,
you squeeze cobalt straight from the tube
and smear it with a palette knife:
blue teapot with two white cups attending.

Your feathers brush the night sky
with ultramarine straight from the tube,
or else, mixed with a medium
of charcoal, spit, and masticated pulp.

Ratcheting left and right,
you strike a Blue Tip match on chert
and fulminate—*burnt, flagrant, phlegm*.

Alert in your devotion,
unseen by any human eye,
you weave a bower of endless night
and pause within, head cocked
to nudge one azure bead
until magnetically aligned,
fussing over vestiges of sky.

ACKNOWLEDGMENTS

These poems have previously appeared in *The Australian*, *Australian Poetry Journal*, *Grey*, *Jubilat*, *Literary Imagination*, *The New Republic*, *The New Yorker*, *The Paris Review*, *Plume*, *Poetry*, *Poetry Northwest*, and *Stolen Island*, and on www.poets.org. "Saturday Morning" was published as a broadside by All Along Press. An earlier version of "Owl-Eyed" appeared in *Telepathy* (Paper Bark Press, 2001).

A few echoes may warrant attribution: "A Fly from the Early Anglers" draws on Gervase Markham and Izaak Walton, among others. "Bright Thorn" quotes *excrucior* from poem 85 of Catullus. "Night and Day" borrows some phrases from Johann Wolfgang von Goethe's *Theory of Colors*. "Ting" quotes a line from Henry Kendall's poem "Bell-Birds": "By channels of coolness the echoes are calling." "Satin Bowerbird" adapts a line from William Blake's "Auguries of Innocence": "Weaves a Bower in endless Night."